Geographic

A Memoir of Time and Space

Geographic

A Memoir of Time and Space

Miriam Sagan

Casa de Snapdragon LLC
Albuquerque, NM

Library of Congress Cataloging-in-Publication Data
Sagan, Miriam, 1954-
Geographic : a memoir of time and space / Miriam Sagan. -- First edition.
    pages cm
Includes bibliographical references and index.
Summary: "Miriam Sagan has written a book that tells in poetic beauty the often difficult and frequently uplifting history of her own life and challenges as she tumbles through the mixture of events that helped contribute to the writer that she is today" -- Provided by publisher.
    ISBN 978-1-937240-62-2 (pbk. : alk. paper) 1. Sagan, Miriam, 1954- 2. Poets, American--20th century--Biography. 3. Life change events. 4. Autobiographical memory. 5. Santa Fe (N.M.)--Biography. I. Title. II. Title: Memoir of time and space.

PS3569.A288Z46 2015
811'.54--dc23
[B]

                              2015028497

20160130
Casa de Snapdragon LLC
12901 Bryce Avenue NE
Albuquerque, NM 87112
Printed in the United States of America

Acknowledgments:

"External Soul" and "House of God" first appeared in *Avatar*

"The Poet in New York" first appeared in *82 Review*

"Lung Tap" in *The Camel Salon*

"Spiral Jetty" first appeared in *Santa Fe Poetry Broadside* and then in the anthology *Just Outside The Frame* (Tres Chicas Books).

"Yaddo" in *Connotation*

"Start Anywhere" was part of a sculptural installation with ceramic artist Christy Hengst at 516 Gallery in Albuquerque. The piece then migrated to the Santa Fe Botanical Garden, winter 2013-14.

Many of these pieces were first-test-driven on my blog Miriam's Well (http://miriamswell.wordpress.com). A big thank you to my readers.

Special thanks to the Center for Land Use Interpretation's Wendover residency, where this book was begun, and for continued inspiration and a way of seeing.

The poems in *Song of the Lark* are taken directly from Willa Cather's novel. Words have been cut, but not added.

Thanks too to Kate McCahill, for her sensitive editing.

And gratitude as always to Richard Feldman.

Contents

Advice

"There is no situation so terrible you can't take a Greyhound bus away from it." My Father

The Wards

In my childhood, the town I grew up in was divided into four wards which were bisected by the shape of a lowercase t. It still is, but the wards are less meaningful, or segregated, than they were fifty years ago. Then, the First Ward was wealthy, WASP-y, and voted Republican. The Second Ward included Jews like my family and some Democrats. The Third Ward was liberal and working-class to middle-class, and the Fourth Ward was African-American and Democratic. Railroad tracks divided the town, intersecting the central avenue. You could cross from ward to ward—my grandparents were in the Third Ward—and I had friends in all four. But the differences there were felt.

I left the Second Ward with caution.

Today the town is prosperous, ethnically varied, essentially a Manhattan suburb but still retaining the essence of New Jersey. My parents' neighbors are no longer old English and Dutch families, but Orthodox Jews who walk to the local synagogue. My parents remain rooted in, and yet quintessentially apart from, the neighborhood. In the 1960s, when we marched as family against the war in Viet Nam, my father used to like to march behind the sign proclaiming: EAST VILLAGE DEMOCRATS AGAINST THE WAR. There was no such sign, of course uniting the denizens of the Second Ward.

The street is gracious and tree-lined. In my teenage years I became aware of what lay behind the screened porches and cupolas—adultery, addiction, incest, suicide, and more. As an adult I see it as no worse, but certainly no better, than any other place where appearances are kept up to the detriment of a confrontation with the truth.

I know too that in some ways I am completely of this place. I did leave the day after I graduated from high school. And yet wherever I am, I want to know the grid, the boundary lines. I want to know where I am, and what it means. In that knowledge I presume some safety; in its absence—danger.

It has been years since I dreamed I flew over the neighborhood, opening the window, pushing off from the sill, floating over the grove of copper beeches, flying over the ward, east to the Hudson River, hanging for a moment over the George Washington Bridge and the glittering Manhattan skyline, which of course was my real life destination. But in this dream I turned left, flew north up Route 9W, upriver, as if towards Canada, Hudson Bay, cold in darkness.

Fleeing the Nazis at the Riverdale Ice Skating Rink

I spent my childhood being terrified of Nazis. Oh, I was afraid of the Cossacks my grandparents ran from, and from the Russians who had missiles aimed right at my elementary school desk, but really it was my parents' terror that haunted me the most. So, Nazis.

Being a practical child, I did fantasize solutions. Where would I hide? How would I run? Every Sunday morning in winter for many years, my father took us to the ice skating rink in Riverdale. I loved it there—the ice, the music, the hot chocolate, the bells and pompoms on my toes. Thanks to a weekly lesson with a guy named Vinnie, I was a pretty good ice skater.

So what did I think about as I skated round and round? Not a figure skating competition with me in an outfit. Not Holland, where I'd glide with Hans Brinker and his silver skates. No, Nazis. I'd skate to the music, all the while fleeing from storm troopers. Of course, on an ice skating rink, you can't really escape. So, mind following feet, I was trapped in a loop.

Once, coming back from the rink when I was nine, we heard the report—Jack Ruby shooting Lee Harvey Oswald. There was an ad on the radio—"Who was the first to conquer space? Castro convertible!" Only years later did I realize the joke. We lived in a prim world where beds were beds and couches did not open. But Castro I knew, on an island that had missiles pointing at it or from it...It didn't surprise me that he was now in the furniture business.

Not in Ideas

When I began as a writer, I didn't have ideas about poetry. I just wanted it. Wanted it to want me.

William Carlos Williams said: No ideas but in things.

Wallace Stevens: Not ideas about the thing but the thing itself.

Schools, concepts, fads meant nothing to me. I simply read everything. Dryden. Ferlinghetti. Sappho. I had no ideas.

But despite these, there are poetic ideas that are not simply matters of aesthetics.

The first real idea I ever heard expressed came from John Malcolm Brinnin when I was in graduate school. He wore fuzzy booties. He was also—unusual in academia—honest about life. I admired everything about him.

He spoke about Merce Cunningham and John Cage. He said—some art forms move in space, some in time.

Sculpture in space.

Poetry in time.

So how to make a poem move in space.

It didn't occur to me to work it calligraphically on the page, to create an open field of indentations and margins.

I wasn't thinking about space in that way.

Rather, I was trying for a Cubist effect within the poem, as if walking around the image (the object + feeling).

A poetic idea isn't about craft (despite the fact that the

word also means a method of transportation). Or subject matter.

I think of it as a description of reality. A map.

Books on My Head: The Nudie Beach

When I was young, my sisters and I liked to go to the nudie beach on Martha's Vineyard—Jungle Beach, as it was then called. This was so long ago that it was before the town of Chilmark opened Lucy Vincent's Beach, and incorporated an au natural section.

To get to Jungle Beach you had to either hack your way overland through poison ivy, or walk the preferred route about 40 minutes oceanside along clay cliffs.

So we set off, carrying provisions, beach chairs, water. I was carrying three fat books by George Eliot: *The Mill on The Floss, Adam Bede,* and *Middlemarch.* I have no idea, from this remove, why I needed all three. Was I perhaps writing a thesis on the beach? Afraid we'd get stranded for months—or years? This was thousands of pages of Victorian novel, all hardback, tiny print, from the library.

Wrapped in a beach towel that modesty dictated for the trip I balanced the three hardbacks on my head with one hand. Came around a multicolored cliff, slipped on a mud slide, and lost the books in the ocean. Scrabbling, I retrieved them, but alas, too late. The pages were salty, wet, and swollen.

And the library fines were pretty hefty, too.

Time

Time itself is a silent partner in all creative enterprise—sometimes feared or destructive, always necessary.

If the poem is like a stalactite, being built up drop by drop. Or even if the process is a mad rush time-lapsed version of the same—slow or fast, it is built in and of time.

To begin is to accept mortality.

To continue is to fear a permanent interruption.

A composer I know said it is always sad to end, even if on a happy note. Because it is over. And then silence.

Image

When I was in high school I was in the foyer of a New York City apartment building where there was a small plot of vividly green grass growing in the lobby. I believe my friend and former camp counselor Peter Frank, who became a well-known curator and art critic, lived there.

Years later, I wondered if it had been a dream, and I asked him. "Oh yes, that must have been..." he said, naming an address I couldn't really remember.

It made an enormous impression on me.

Manhattan

In northern New Jersey, there are two distinct places: New Jersey and Manhattan. From New Jersey to the city flows fear and desire, longing and envy. Also, a kind of studied scorn.

From the city towards New Jersey there is complete indifference.

No wonder I'm obsessed with space, and with buses #84 and #86, which will take me across the George Washington Bridge.

I was born in Manhattan and my family moved when I was four. I am trying to get back. However, when I gain a modicum of freedom in my twenties I'll go west. Turns out I'm an American after all.

How much of my family must I describe? My parents had wealth and education, liberal politics. They were both good-looking. They were certainly of their generation.

Two young people, they met on a blind date that didn't take, then on a trolley car.

Between the two of them, they feared much of human life and this world, and raged.

An astrologer told me: the family you were born into was already sad.

The long polished hallway. The scarred underside of a kitchen table. My terror of the interior of certain houses.

Here is the dark side of my coin, the faceless side, flip tails.

I believe in chance, not astrology.

But this reading of the stars was correct.

It was already sad.

No wonder I care about space.

lower level

The night that Martha opened, my mother put us in the station wagon in our pajamas and drove us across the George Washington Bridge. Then turned around and drove back where the seal of the Great State of New York turned into that of the Great State of New Jersey. We yelled and threw flower petals plucked from our garden out the window. The bridge spanned two shores, two worlds. Beautiful like all suspension bridges, it had been built by fearless Mohawk steelworkers. I walked across it a few times with boyfriends. If my mother really hated a friend of mine she'd say: if J. told you to jump off the George Washington Bridge, would you jump?

Yes, I'd say. I'd jump.

What Could Be Closed

The lid of the music box. When opened, the tiny ballerina spun in her starched tutu in front of a mirror. Velvet-lidded compartments awaited precious trinkets.

A book.
The piano—although it was not.
The locked door of my parents' bedroom.
My closet.
A zipper.
An umbrella.
Windows.
The tiny door leading to a crawl space beyond the attic.

A shell containing Japanese paper flowers which would open if placed in a bowl of water. And could not be shut again.
My mouth.
An empty cigar box.
The house's library door, me inside on an ottoman, being lectured on my poor performance in school.
Feeling.
A locket.
Buttons.
Snaps.
Scissors.
A paper cut.
Both my eyes.

The Poet in New York

When I was a teenager, my father drew his own map on the map of Manhattan—indicating where I was and was not allowed to go. He trusted me, and with reason—I complied. I was not allowed on the subway until I was fifteen. As a result, my path to midtown or the West Village or Sheep's Meadow looked like this: walk to the NJ bus that would drop me at the George Washington Bridge at 179th Street and then take the Number 4 bus from Washington Heights to Harlem and then downtown to wherever I was going to meet my friends.

The Number 4 bus was both an education and transportation—proof of Montaigne's directive that the journey, not the arrival, matters. It was utterly fascinating. Hassids, black people, white people, Indian ladies in saris marred by winter coats, people speaking Spanish, hip and scary teenagers, old people...all rode together.

Harlem was not technically on my allowed map, but I devoured its sights from the bus—churches, Nation of Islam storefronts, Black Power bookstores, Sugar Hill, and, since the route was mostly Broadway, fruit and vegetable markets. Imagine me a suburban teenager in purple maxi coat and cute but not snow-worthy boots, dangling screw-on earrings, zits. At fifteen I'd be taking the A train and offering my seat to anyone infirm or pregnant, but at fourteen I was finding my urban legs.

The Number 4 bus always felt secure, no matter what

block it was passing through. The bus drivers in NYC in the 1960s seemed a tough breed to me, captains of their ships. I knew nothing bad would happen to me in their presence. But I also made a point of sitting next to whatever kindly-looking lady of any race or ethnicity I could find. I'd smile at said lady, and most often she'd smile back.

Enter Federico Garcia Lorca.

There was a wonderful bookstore at the George Washington Bridge, heavy on the New Directions paperbacks. I read Kenneth Rexroth's translations from the Chinese. Anais Nin. And then I discovered my lifelong love—Lorca. Forget that he was gay—and dead. I was madly in love with my first poetry boyfriend. Until I had the shock of reading "A Poet In New York." A masterpiece, quintessential, revered...what upset me was that I thought of New York as MINE.

"How come Lorca gets to write about New York?" I asked myself over and over. At fourteen, I didn't realize the question was ludicrous, or the answer simple—poets get to write about whatever they want. I think what upset me was that I'd been BORN in Manhattan, and spent the better part of my life, age 12-14, on the Number 4 bus. But Lorca seemed to know more than I did about what I was seeing. How was this possible?

My much younger self seems endearingly stupid now—Lorca was of course many things I was not—a grown-up, a genius, a full-fledged poet. But my seemingly foolish response helped me immeasurably in the years to come.

First of all, it gave me permission. I could write about anything, anywhere. I didn't have to write what I "knew"—I could write from unknowing, or simple observation. Second of all, it gave me a goal I could never reach—to write a poem as beautiful. These two things have given me as much pleasure as anything else I have found in life.

I do have to say, though, that I've never written a poem about the Number 4 bus.

More Advice

"(The poet) must leave New Jersey." Clement Greenberg quoted in Ann Reynolds's book *Robert Smithson: Learning from New Jersey and Elsewhere.*

After Robert Smithson

you can navigate
by a lighthouse
or the constellations
by a map of broken glass
clear jagged panes
heaped up
to form a lost continent

what if this
is really New Jersey
with its riot-shattered storefronts
its burning
garbage-heaped meadowlands
what if New Jersey is Atlantis

Smithson

Time makes ruins of monuments.

The Acropolis, Petra, Chaco, an Esso gas station.

The New Jersey of my childhood contained every conceivable item in the grab bag of samsara.

And no one seemed remotely interested in it.

Enter Robert Smithson (although it turns out that he was already there—and already dead and gone by the time I noticed).

Smithson called New Jersey "The Crystal Land." As a child, I once spent an entire day looking at my world through a prism which outlined each familiar and mundane scene in rainbows.

Smithson looked in the rearview mirror, and explored surveyor's space—which is simply a map. Or not so simply.

He liked fragile marks—a stamp on a postcard.

He built Spiral Jetty—a massive earthwork—in the Great Salt Lake. I knew what he knew—that at the Jersey shore jetties were built to break the ocean's force.

Those jetties broke space.

Spiral Jetty, in a waveless lost inland sea, could only have been constructed to break time.

Spiral Jetty

Robert Smithson
1938-1973

A man builds an enormous ramp
then wants to see it from the air

he's thirty-five, the plane will crash
his view of a darkness entering the skull

building a jetty in the shape of a fiddlehead fern
gelatin-silver print of the great salt lake

facade covered in shells
statue of a neoclassical figure, draped

like a madonna against a bathtub turned upright
egg blue planted with roses and petunias

"the slurb": industrial and suburban
cattail marsh, geese, floating oil slick

that dark place by the river
intersection of muggers and grass-stained lovers

graffiti: PASSAIC BOYS ARE HELL
(but aren't we all)

ruined motel, and how we will live in it
walls without roof

bed without walls
floor without bed

you without me...
someone set mirrors in the snow

a trail of mirrors
accurately reflecting...snow

"as soon as it was named
it ceased to exist"

spiral jetty on the lake
body of water without a tidal shore

body of water without encroaching wave
water like the level of a dream

after his father's death
after his lost brother

he thought: the jetty is down
there is nothing between me and death...

abandoned quarry full of water
"an oval map of a double world"

his pediatrician, the famous poet
looked down his throat to find the aleph

looked in the waxy labyrinth of his ear
the body's chambers are discreet

only in childhood do we regret
the swallowed cherry pit that will not sprout and bloom

green branch exiting my mouth
laden red with Eden

ramp, mirror, edge
road map crumpled on the motel floor

we squinted so long at
it appeared eventually

no map of destination
but a map of stars

Site

There is a need for an object, that is, a site, in order to write a poem. Originally for me that starting point was experience, feeling, the body. But this changed dramatically when I started working more directly with land. This became a different way of writing, based off location (time/space) rather than on something purely personal that was usually record or memory.

This helped to stop feeling that I was commoditizing experience: widowhood=widow poems=widow poems performance=an unpleasant objectification of self.

There was nothing wrong with the earlier process—it is the poet's process—but it was a tremendous relief when it changed.

To have an idea and not be a prisoner of the idea.

I hear Joan Sutherland-Roshi say that kensho can only come from outside the self—the guttural caw of a crow or Venus rising as the morning star. It doesn't arise from anyone's inner authenticity.

So, sorry to say, the New Age, self-help, diet, exercise, even therapy—these may lead to a brushed-up version of the self but they won't lead to a poem.

The poem comes from outside—hence the muse. Hence what I am seeking.

Robert Smithson says there are two sites—the original one and the gallery or museum piece. In my case the second site is the poem.

At DIA Beacon I saw the enormous metal holding tanks of sculpture by Richard Serra. I'd never liked them before—too industrial—but in this space these were like mazes or kivas—as well as New Jersey industrial wasteland.

I saw Smithson's heaps of earth from specific places piled up on the floor, holding up mirrors. To this world.

Apocryphal Advice

"Space is the corpse of time." Robert Smithson

Panama

When I was in the fifth grade, I had to write a report about Panama. I was not very good at this kind of thing, and the report got a B, which was basically unacceptable in my family. How would I get into Harvard?

Panama made no sense to me. I could not locate it. I copied out various facts onto lined paper and glued two colored pictures of butterflies to the end.

I could not locate myself in relationship to Panama. That year I got briefly locked in the girls' bathroom avoiding tumbling class and had to bang on the door for a few panicky moments.

I did not like tumbling, putting my head between my knees in a posture of emergency and rolling forward.

I liked the classical world, the gods of Greece and Rome, where time had turned monuments to ruins.

I liked the fragile marks of sandpiper tracks, stamps of exotic birds and fruits on postcards, cattail marshes and refinery flames in the rearview mirror.

If I was standing, where was Panama? South meant below me, but where—my feet?

In fifth grade, a bad boy named Mark stabbed my friend Karo with a sharpened pencil, right into her luscious white upper arm, and made her bleed. I don't think he was punished much—boys weren't in those days.

Or so I remember. Other classmates remember that a boy was stabbed, not a girl.

A year later, time made me bleed into my underpants at a double feature of *A Hard Day's Night* and *Help!* An afternoon with the Beatles tipped me into puberty and soon I no longer cared at all about Panama.

Even More Advice

"Immense is not an object." Bachelard

Poetics of Space

My poem does not move in space. It moves in time. It maddens me, just lying there, like a fillet of fish I don't want to even bother cooking.

On the bookshelf is a copy of Bachelard's *Poetics of Space.*

I am alone in an apartment in suburban northern California, housesitting for some friends. I am "writing." I am in my mid-twenties, unmarried, unemployed, and unpublished.

There is a warning that the fruit trees will be sprayed with Paraquat. I stay inside.

But a bad urinary tract infection sends me to the ER. I take a bus. The young woman doctor prescribes antibiotics, then notes the huge scar on my thorax from lung surgery five years ago. I also have a fresh burn on one leg from a motorcycle tailpipe.

"You're leading an exciting life," she says.

A misdiagnosis.

Malpais

When I was twenty-one years old, I almost died. I had, what in retrospect must have been swine flu—an influenza that went to my lungs, collapsed them, gave me pleurisy and then empyema. I spent several months in the Beth Israel hospital, where my life was saved.

Thirty-six years later, I was sitting in a cafe with my friend Kathleen when I found myself saying: "My soul is in a jar in the basement of the B.I."

"Then you'd better go get it," she said.

A little while later, she added, "I wonder if you love rough, harsh, remote places because of being in the hospital."

Bad lands.

1. Beth Israel Hospital

A scar runs through it...

the Beth Israel Hospital
like a giant ship
lit up on a snowy winter's night
its prow illuminated
curving into a rough sea,
the slum of the Fenway
Boston sprawled out beneath it
hookers, hipsters, gangbangers, projects
and ordinary people
going home to cook dinner

meanwhile I'm tossed
in my berth
of a hospital bed
across an inner storm
of fever and infection
raging across the
twenty-one-year-old thing
that used to be
my body.

2. Lung Tap

my name is on my wrist
so it has come to this

there's screaming down the hall
but why I can't recall

they say the screamer is me
but this is hard to see

I tell her to shut up
scream lessens not a bit

my name is on my wrist
an opiate of bliss

in sacrificial pose
bound knees support my nose

the needle is my name
she's screaming just the same

I read what I am called
and memory is jarred

my name is on my wrist
m-i-r-i-a-m means bitterness

3. The Gypsies

In a hospital room just a few doors down from mine
Patriarch propped in bed
Women in voluminous skirts
Forty people camped in the hall
Eating what smells like
Delicious liverwurst sandwiches
Wrapped in wax paper.

The sole English speaker
A boy, maybe ten
Is pushed forward
To the doctor of the hour—
The old man needs surgery,
Or will recover.
And the child
Hung between English
And the incomprehensible
Translates
Clicking his tongue against his teeth.

How I envy them
Not just the petticoats
And me in my backless
Hospital gown
I envy that they don't speak English
And that they're not alone.

4. What Accompanied Me

the Jamaican night aide, who would turn me and tuck
me in
in an hour so black mere loneliness couldn't touch it

my boyfriend, upon whom I performed
not-to-be-described acts
so he wouldn't run around on me
too much,
who also ate heartily
of the Swedish meatballs
and Jell-O on my untouched tray

the plump pretty nurse with red curls
who enviously didn't understand why I cried
each morning on the scale
as I lost my entire
adult weight

the Harvard psychiatric intern
who inquired
"how does it feel
to be 21
and have almost died?"
as I screamed
and threw him out

the corpse
of the black lady
who was briefly
my roommate

the pitcher of water
I poured on myself
by mistake
with my ruined right arm,
and my own coat
that I slept under
because I could not
get a change of sheets
that last night in the hospital.

5. Patty Hearst

I was dying but I did not die
And Patty Hearst got caught
Rich girl posturing as a revolutionary
Yes, she had my sympathy
Locked in a closet, beaten
God knows what else
Scared out of her Daddy's little girl wits
And now a radical, temporarily.

I sympathized until I heard the nurses talk
They cursed Patty, saying
The rich bitch should not get off
I was afraid
They'd think the same ill of me
I wasn't working class, or Irish
But somehow I remained their pet
They'd wash my hair in a basin
Braid it
Until I looked like I was twelve years old again.

But it was only years later
That I understood
They were the last in a line
Of tough smart women
Who didn't get to go to med school
(their daughters surely would)

And they liked me anyway
Despite their buried rage
And they pitied me
Sometimes even with a tear
For being just their age.

6. The External Soul

break an egg
dot the corners of the house
with viscous albumen
to draw back the soul
that has crept like a cat
beneath the threshold
of the
unendurable

7. *House of God*

Thirty-six years later
I return to Boston
Where my life was saved
And I acquired
A terror
Of finding myself
In a human body.

(and if it was contagious
if it was
redeemable)

Where was beauty
Where had it been
In the damp cold
When I'd bought
A paper butterfly kite
From Chinatown
And hung it
Over the four poster bed
That had been my mother's.

A loneliness
More bitter than black bread
Or old coffee
Seized beneath my breast bone.

Siren in the night—
The simple fear
That I'd die
In a ward
Of a great city hospital
In the snow
Without ever once
Having left
This place.

Yaddo

When I was 25, I spent a month at Yaddo in dead winter. There were only a few residents. And three records for the record player.

1. Edith Sitwell, the poet, reading her pretentious British-accented fake jazzy lines.

2. Bird calls of North America

3. Steve Reich's "Music for 18 Musicians."

We'd actually play them over and over, smoking pot and lying on the floor in hysterics over Sitwell's intonations.

The Reich was beautiful, a grid of sound like plaid or city streets. Over and over it tried to tell me both that I should run and that I was impossibly connected to every-thing:

pink glass lanterns glowing at dusk

a cold wind out of Canada

Saratoga's hot dark bubbling springs

ghosts of my life poised momentarily in a doorway

I tried to read *The Brothers Karamazov* and failed. I wrote a few poems I didn't like. I caught cold.

If only I had believed then what the music told me—that people would love me, that I'd have my own house and a flowered skirt that brushed my ankles.

I retained nothing of the bird calls.

even today

I don't know that note
or what bird.

Nancy Holt

I identify with Nancy Holt because she and I were both married to men named Robert who died in their mid-thirties.

However, her husband was Robert Smithson.

Her work fascinates me because so much of it is about location.

We lived for a time in the same town, we know people in common, but when I hear her lecture I sit in the back and am overcome with shyness when she signs my copy of her book.

I publish poems about her, but am too embarrassed to send them to her.

I hardly ever idolize someone but she seems "real" in some kind of luminous movie star way, although rationally I assume she is quite ordinary.

She is my tie to a mythic age of heroic artistic endeavor, but more than that, her work shocked the hell out of me. I did not know that anyone could think like that—a way I am perilously close to thinking myself.

I walk in her piece, Dark Star Park, in suburban Virginia with my second husband and my recently widowed father-in-law. Although the sculptural installation is about location in time, to me it also seems to be about grief.

A yahrzeit is the Hebrew date of a death's anniversary.

Every year, I unknowingly pass the day of my own

death. When younger, I passed dates I couldn't yet see—of my lost virginity, of the terrible car crash my daughter survived, of the day we got the two kittens from the animal shelter.

I have never seen Holt's iconic work, Sun Tunnels, although I was close. I was living in a tiny trailer out on the salt flats in Utah, in the abandoned Wendover air force base. Easy to say, but not that easy to do—scary, windy, desolate. It was a residency with the Center for Land Use Interpretation. I was sharing the trailer with Eva, a young photographer from East Berlin.

She was young enough that the wall coming down was history. We were glad of the company at night, both of us nervous.

A rainy day, creatively dull, east Nevada blacked-out for electrical repair work. We thought about heading to Sun Tunnels but ended up on mining roads that Eva was photographing and in a redneck bar that she, no American woman, assumed would be fine—which, surprisingly, it was. We drank cold coffee and when the lights came on treated ourselves to a steak dinner in the local casino.

A year later we crossed paths for an instant—I arrived at the trailer for the second stay of my residency as Eva, car packed, was leaving. I spent a week completely alone in the rattling wind. All fear had left me. I was calm and happy in a direct confrontation with this world as it was. I looked at the sun too long and burned a retinal image on my vision—a tiny image of the sun that projected itself everywhere I looked for over an hour.

Eva was headed for Sun Tunnels on her way home.

Locator

After Nancy Holt

pattern of stars
cast
inside the concrete tunnels

shadow of the sculpture
falls on the exact date
of your anniversary

location
is also about time
as is a telescope

you look much younger
in the photograph

the poles shift
more frequently
than a lot of things

the novelty
of Polaris
as North Star

don't look directly at the sun
or drink
from the sculpture garden's fountains

steps, staircase
vanishing point
of the past

and she was weaving
a pattern of a star
over Chaco

like seeing one's own eyelashes
surveyor
incidental

we look happy
in the photograph

Alignment

A childless woman builds a tunnel of suns
And spends the rest of her life
Photographing it

You ask yourself
What it is possible
To recover from

An array of potholes
One for each
Visible planet

Where a woman will crouch in labor
Display the umbilical cord
Of a king

Now full of water
Now dry
Now reflective...now empty

A Geographic

Mental health worker slang, as in "they pulled a geographic." As in, "Those junkies should have gone into rehab but instead they just moved to Vermont, hoping that would work." As in: changing one's location instead of solving one's problems.

Map Dot Fingerprint Dystrophy

What luck! I have a disease
With the word "map" in it
And apparently
Large slightly gray outlines
Like continents on a globe
Etched on my cornea
(was it too much
sightseeing?)
Concentric circles
Like a fingerprint
As if
I'd put my finger
On the atlas
Of my eye.
Retinal afterimage,
Ghost or optical
Illusion,
Persistence of vision,
Lock and key,
A mushroom cloud
Negative
On the eyelid.
I also have
I've been told
A geographic tongue

Also called topographic
So I bought a little shrine
Of a porcelain doll
In a sardine can
Dressed in a map
Dangling
An airplane
And a tiny globe
To try and settle down.

Christic in the Desert

The first time I was at Christ in the Desert monastery it was winter, 1985, a wet and early Lent. I'd been told it was a good place to write, so my husband Robert drove me in our ancient Dodge Aspen. The road was not frequently graded in those days, and the car sank in the caliche mud. We pried it out, using wooden boards lifted from an old corral, only to have the brakes fail.

We ditched the car and started to walk. It was dusk. We had no idea how far we were, but soon enough saw the church and its cross rising ahead. A very ancient feeling— coming out of wilderness to a monastery.

Indeed, there was hot soup and a general country interest in our car problems. As we were married, the monks gave us one cell with a narrow single bed to share. I had to talk the guest master into giving us a second cell. He looked perplexed that we didn't want to share.

Snow cleared, tractors headed out, Robert cruised the car to the nearest town. I stayed enclosed, with a wood stove and lantern. I knew nothing about this country, having come from San Francisco, and before that Boston and New Jersey. There were a few guests, less than a dozen brothers. The heater in the church was broken. The greenhouse/cold porch off the old convento served for prayer and library.

Suddenly it was St. Patrick's Day—whiskey, meat, laughter. Then I was supposed to leave. Huge storms swept in, covering the Chama River gorge. A hermit—brother Xavier—and a woman anchorite would appear from time to time out of the snow.

I was very far away in time and space from what I knew...Why had I actually gone to Christ in the Desert? To be sure, I was looking for something. I was thirty years old, and a failure as a Buddhist. I couldn't sit still, that hallmark of Soto Zen. When I crossed my legs for zazen, I would shake violently. But my husband Robert wanted to be a Zen priest. We'd left a scandal-ridden San Francisco Zen Center to come to New Mexico. Phil Whalen, beat poet and Zen monk, had simply banned me from the zendo. It was a negative introduction to a man I would come to adore. I was fifty before I realized what a great favor he had inadvertently done me. So there I was, unable to practice Zen and totally unacquainted with the Judaism of my birth. It would be years before I found a woman Hassidic teacher and studied Hebrew and Torah with her.

I was adrift. Monasticism was one of the virtues esteemed in my marriage—ridiculously contradictory as that now sounds. So I found myself in a monastery, a Catholic one to be sure, but this was a religion I was basically neutral towards. I liked reading the psalms, before I ever learned the Jewish practice of reciting them. I liked the two big dogs that followed the abbot everywhere.

Towards the spectacular red rock canyon that enclosed me in a larger version of a monk's cell I felt an awe tinged with respect—an attitude that would serve me well as I came to know New Mexico. In the evening between Vespers and Compline, I walked the deeply rutted road south of the monastery as if walking home. But of course turned back after a few miles. I walked with a young woman about my age whose name I no longer remember. We used dead branches as walking sticks. Once on the road, we felt free to talk. She was trying to become a nun, but was stymied in some way. It was partly to do with her openness about her previous romantic history. In this, she reminded me of Thomas Merton.

I do wonder what became of her. She was more adventurous than I was, a solitary person. Sometimes we saw a coyote, but the packs kept their distance on the other side of the river.

What did I do all short winter's day? I wrote the longest poem I had ever written, but I was also editing the complete poetry of Anna Akhmatova, eventually published by Zephyr Press. I read Mary Stewart's trilogy about Merlin as battered paperbacks left in the guest common room. And I worked the Akhmatova—perfectly suited for the environment—full of candles, nuns, snow, and suffering. I puzzled over the word "faience." Convinced it was obscure, and lacking a dictionary, I had no idea what it was and circled it in red, only to fall prey to the translator's wrath. It was a perfectly fine word for a pottery glaze. I just didn't know it. The snow cleared. A guest with front-wheel drive took me out. She was a professional woman from Albuquerque who drove with ferocious precision, looking coiffed and ironed even after a stay in mud season.

I went home.

I have returned to C in the D three times since then for short stays. Now the Coleman lanterns are battery charged, the stoves gas. This summer's day it is busy, with some visitors just stopping in for a few hours on that road I once found impassable. There are goldfinches, magpies, lizards, butterflies, and silence. It is still a place like no other, but it is not the place I first encountered. I cannot find that again, even as I cannot reclaim the thirty-year-old me.

So much has happened, and perhaps so little. I have been to many remote places to write. But even today I am writing in a brocade notebook, just like the ones I used to buy in San Francisco's Chinatown.

That first stay here did do one thing—it turned me from a failed Buddhist into a New Mexican. It changed what I feared, what I admired. It did not give me what I was looking for, but it gave me a way to keep looking.

Cut Up

I took a big scissors and cut up Willa Cather's novel *The Song of the Lark.*

The Song of the Lark

after Willa Cather

#1

Seen from a balloon
Moonstone looked like a Noah's Ark town
Set out in the sand
Lightly shaded by tamarisks
And cottonwoods. The frail
Brightly painted desert town
Was shaded
By the light-reflecting
Wind-loving trees whose roots
Are always seeking water
Whose leaves
Are always talking about it
Making the sound of rain.

The roots
Break into wells
And thieve the water.

#2

She took up one of the white conch shells
that bordered the walk
and held it to his ear.
"You hear something in there?
You hear the sea; and yet
the sea is very far from here.
You have judgment, but if you are fooled
it is the sea itself."

The sound startled.
It was like something
calling one.

#3

There was a picture
her picture
nobody cared for it
it waited for her.

That was a picture indeed
"The Song of the Lark"
flat country, early
morning light
wet fields, the look
in the girl's heavy face.

They were all hers.

The picture was "right"
a word that covered
the almost boundless satisfaction
she felt
when she looked at the picture.

Whatever was there
was all hers.

#4

There were a great many trains
dashing east and west
on the face of the continent,
all carried young people
who meant to have things.
But the difference was
that she was going to get them!
At that early hour there were few people
in the dining car.
On each table was a slender vase
with a single pink rose in it
recklessly offering its yellow heart.

#5

The moonlight
was so bright

The moonflowers wide open
and of an unearthly white

The moon itself
looked like

A great pale flower
in the sky

#6

more than the mountain disappeared,

the personality—of which
she was so tired—
seemed
to let go of her,
high, sparkling air
drank it up
like blotting paper

so far, she had failed
in the essential things
she had made no advance
her life
closed behind her
like the forest

#7

Panther Canyon
an abrupt fissure
with which the earth
in the Southwest
is riddled

perpendicular cliffs
striped
with ever-running
strata of rock

in this hollow
like a great fold
the Ancient People
built their houses
of yellowish stone
and mortar

the dead city
lay
at the point
where the perpendicular
outer wall ceased
and the V-shaped
inner gorge
began.

#8

Here she could lie
undistracted
holding
pleasant and incomplete
conceptions in her mind—
almost in her hands
something to do with fragrance
color
sound

Music had never come to her
in that sensuous form before
she could become
a mere receptacle
like the bright lizards
that darted about
on the hot stones
she could become a continuous repetition of sound
like the cicadas

#9

The stream was the only living thing
left of the drama
that had been played out in the canyon
centuries ago.

What was any art
but an effort to make a sheath, a mold
in which to imprison for a moment
the shining, elusive life hurrying past us.

Along the trails, under the spreading cactus
there still glittered in the sun
bits of frail clay vessels,
fragments of desire.

Is Space Sexy?

I was once in a very odd motel with a man I loved very much. This was in Marathon Key, Florida, where every inlet or boat dock commanded the marketing advertisement of "water view." Multicolored fairy lights were wrapped around the trunks of palm trees. A modest room with an adequate bed and a cool breeze through the window.

Another room, huge, empty of furniture but for four gigantic refrigerators along with noisy freezers, compressors wrenching off and on. For game fish, no doubt, but useless to us.

I knew you were worried about something, but I didn't know what. Turns out it was a relatively minor fixable pain, but you were concerned that it was something more frightening. You didn't yet want to talk about it.

The motel room was ugly and odd, but I was happy there with you. Perhaps that was when I truly realized how much I loved you.

I had been in Venice, Italy with a man and felt less, trapped within a postcard of expectations, something static I had to feed to keep alive.

Dusk comes suddenly and swiftly in the subtropics. At exact sea level, the Key roiled with fish at its margins, the colored lights blinking.

Playboy of the Western World

I remember sitting in the theater when I was a teenager, waiting for the play to begin, in Manhattan, midtown, Broadway.

It must have been a school trip. The play was by the Irish writer, John Synge. I didn't know anything about it, except that it was a comedy, set in the west of Ireland and about a young man who thinks he has killed his father, and as a result becomes irresistible to women.

I sat in the audience and as the house lights came down and the theater quieted something very surprising happened to me. I felt awash in a sea of vastness, like a grain of sand on the shore of some huge dark ocean, cold swirls coming in from outer space, a profound hush. I was overwhelmed, a little frightened. It was like drinking very sweet water or being awake and asleep at the same time.

The curtain went up. The ancient sea receded and the action began.

I wanted this sensation again, like morphine or love. I searched for it in hospital wards and suicide hotlines, Boston and San Francisco, Zen centers and yoga classes, in the arms of strangers and husbands, in the faces of children and bus drivers, theories of physics and bars on upper Polk Street, rain, snow and mist.

If I find it, I will not tell you. If you find it, show it to me, even just a fossil of its ripples.

Suicide: A Calendar of Water

My bipolar uncle goes off lithium and jumps off the Bay Bridge.

His body floats for several days, and then is picked up by a fishing boat.

The exact date of his death is unknown.

My father decides his brother has killed himself on my father's birthday, March 3.

My father and I walk along the edge of the park where greenery intersects with retail, a pleasant stroll.

"Do you think your family was...unusual..." I venture.

"They were totally average," he says.

"One in three jumped off a bridge," I say.

"Totally average," he says.

We walk into a neighborhood of attractive restaurants and bars.

"How can they name a bar that!" My father exclaims, shocked.

"What?"

He points.

The sign reads: BULLS-hyphen-HEAD.

My father has misread it as "Bullshead," which he pronounces as "Bullshit."

I do understand that everyone needs their own version.

In mine, my uncle has jumped off the Golden Gate.

It just sounds better.

Motherless

If I tell the truth, and not a truth prettied up for consumption, I find very little female influence. And this is despite my desperate yearning for it.

I did not have many mothers.

Lady Liberty might be my mother, or Harriet Tubman, or Sacajawea—but they are not.

Sometimes I tell myself that I am Patti Smith's daughter, the one she gave up for adoption—a biological impossibility given our respective ages.

Women move in space, at least the female body does, wrapped in a bath towel, or naked, or a nude.

You'd think I would like that.

But I do not.

My mother wanted to be a writer, but she did not want to write. She tried in her twenties, and ended up inert in bed.

As a young mother, she continued to want to be a writer. She was working on a short story that engrossed her. She was up in the middle of the night thinking about it. Then she lectured herself: you are a wife and mother. You can't let anything else take your attention.

She threw the story in to the wastebasket, never to be retrieved.

After that, she tried in fits and starts in every successive decade. But it did not work.

The Muse was thinking: this is no way to treat a lady.

Time Peace

April 27, 1954

Iam born, by natural childbirth, in Mt. Sinai Hospital in New York City. My mother delivers me a little after 3 p.m., after the nurses' shift changes. They are loath to go because they have never seen natural childbirth before.

I am born into a world marked forever by Auschwitz and Hiroshima. Strange how innocent place names can come to speak of universal horror. I am born in upper Manhattan. For my entire life, my dreams will have NY City street signs in them. I will always know the cardinal directions in my dreams.

Manhattan Project, 1942-1946

Robert Oppenheimer and other physicists develop the atom bomb in a remote location in New Mexico—Los Alamos. It is tested in southern New Mexico, in the Jornado del Muerto. As an adult, I visit the Trinity Test Site on one of the two days of the year it is open and buy myself a lavender T-shirt with a blue mushroom cloud on it.

I wear it out.

Cuban Missile Crisis. October, 1962

Our third grade teacher, Mrs. Harvey, is no-nonsense and British. We know she survived the London blitz. She pulls down a map of the world from the blackboard at the front of the class and shows us that Russia practically touches Alaska. They have always been right next door and able to bomb us. For some reason, this banishes my fear.

August 6, 1945

The atom bomb "Little Boy" is dropped on Hiroshima by the U.S. by a plane named Enola Gay. On August 9, "Fat Man" is detonated over Nagasaki by the U.S. by a plane named Bockscar.

November 22, 1963

President John F. Kennedy is assassinated. I am in the fourth grade and miss Mrs. Harvey with her great accent.

This may be the first time I realize my family is different than others. The next school day many kids say they saw their fathers cry. My father did not cry, but he did drink a beer in the daytime while watching television—very unusual behavior.

Years later I learned that Fidel Castro remarked—who is this man Johnson and can he handle the CIA?

My father seemed to be asking some sort of similar question.

Autumn, 1905, Russia

A general strike is called throughout the Tsarist Russia—a revolution, really. My grandfather Avrum, who is a short, skinny teenager, is lifted up by other men so he can pull the whistle which signals the start of the local protest.

April 4, 1968. Martin Luther King Assassination

The house next to us, which is abandoned, burns. It is a vast house with turrets and follies—we call it the pink castle. My parents are away, and my grandfather Avrum and I sit up all night together watching the firemen and keeping an eye so that the strand of copper beeches between us and the conflagration don't catch fire.

November 7, 1867

Madame Sklodowska Curie, discoverer of radium, is born. I read her biography, along with those of Harriet Tubman and Joan of Arc. I will never do what any of them did, but as a girl in the 1950s I take my heroines where I can find them.

November, 1984

I move to Santa Fe, New Mexico a few days after Ronald Reagan wins the election and am amazed to see the lights of Los Alamos twinkling in the northwest. It is as if I did not know it was a real place.

Tisha B'Av, 1492. Jews expelled from Spain

This date, the 9th day of the month of Av, is the least auspicious one on the Hebrew calendar.

The Jews are expelled from Spain, leaving my family with a taste for flamenco and me with the desire to just keep driving south into Mexico.

August 19-21, 1991. Fall of Soviet Union

The coup against Michael Gorbachev fails. During the two days of the attempt, my parents are huddled in the basement of their beach house because a hurricane is devastating the island of Martha's Vineyard.

Periodically my father braves the wind and threat of broken glass to run up the stairs to the kitchen, where he can get good radio reception to find out what is happening in Russia.

9th of Av, 70 CE

The destruction of the Second Temple in Jerusalem. It is commemorated by the Romans on a triumphal arch, still in Rome. The arch of Titus shows the plundered menorah carried off by soldiers. The start of the intensification of Jewish diaspora.

November, 2010. Wendover, Utah

Desert dawn, azure sky. Venus hangs over the guard tower. The lights of the casinos blink reflected in the windows of the Enola Gay hangar. I drink a cup of coffee by myself.

Start Anywhere

I didn't want to be sentimental about the body—yours, mine, or the land's.

When the Twin Towers came down I had been expecting it.

A bridge hung between the two voids.

I had been waiting my whole life for someone to believe what I saw.

A bridge hung between two voids.

There was an autobiography between me and Hiroshima.

You could not take it out of context because there was no context.

It was as if it had happened to me.

The refinery blew up in Elizabeth, New Jersey and I saw the mushroom cloud on the horizon.

I had been waiting for it my whole life.

We never actually hid under our desks at school—I think that was because it was private and not public school. But I had heard about it so often it was as if...

I had been waiting my whole life for someone to believe what I saw.

It was as if it was my fault.

As if it had happened to me.

A blue door leading into a Persian garden.

Final Advice

"I advise you not to return to your native place." Zen Master Mazu Daoyi, Chinese, 8th century

About Miriam Sagan

Miriam Sagan was born in Manhattan, grew up in New Jersey, studied in Boston, and lived on the coastal extremes of Martha's Vineyard and San Francisco before settling in Santa Fe, New Mexico in 1984. She founded and runs the creative writing program at Santa Fe Community College. She is the author of over twenty-five books, including *Searching for a Mustard Seed: A Young Widow's Unconventional Story*, which won a Best Memoir of the Year Award from the Independent Publishers Association. Her travels have taken her to remote locations as a writer-in-residence, including such settings as national parks, sculpture gardens, a trailer in the Great Basin, and Iceland. She has received a Santa Fe Mayor's Award for Excellence in the Arts and the New Mexico Literary Arts Poetry Gratitude Award. Her text installations have included poetry on laundry lines, trees, glass, sculpture, aprons, earrings, sand trays, and haiku street signs. She has also written a poem directly on Miami's South Beach, during a residency at The Betsy Hotel. Her artistic collaborations include working with her daughter, visual artist Isabel Winson-Sagan. She lives with her husband Richard Feldman on Santa Fe's unfashionable west side.

Recent Releases from

JB Stillwater

Casa de Snapdragon LLC

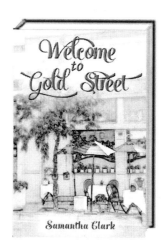

Welcome to Gold Street
Samantha Clark
ISBN: 978-1-937240-54-7
$13.95 Paperback
$4.99 eBook

For Nancy, Gold Street in Albuquerque is a dream come true: a downtown main street where she can open her own store. Her comfortable, yet predictable, life back in a small Midwestern university town was never like this. But did she pick somewhere too different to open a new business?

Nancy quickly depletes her inheritance while setting up her quilt shop, she and her new best friend are torn apart over a man, the other store owners are beyond quirky, and there's disturbing talk about magic on Gold Street. Plus, the locals have the worst habit of polluting their food with spicy green chile. Did Nancy make a mistake?

Fabrytius' Chylde
Lynn Strongin
ISBN: 978-1-937240-56-1
$14.95 Paperback
$4.99 eBook

The dark and the bright light of seventeenth century Holland permeates this love story. This is the light in which Fabrytius, Rembrandt's most illustrious pupil, painted. Is the light his chylde? Or is it the passion between two women in a Boston marriage? We are mystically called forth to decide. It is the story of Angel and Velvet, both theatre buffs and book lovers. How they struggle to overcome a nearly tragic decision in a southern town is revealed. The core of the book is a crisis which, in age, challenges them to rise; a phoenix from the fire rather than swirl in the heavenly chiaroscuro light of seventeenth century Holland, angels in ashes.

86 Sonnets for the 21st Century
Mary Barnet
ISBN: 978-1-937240-50-9
$13.95 Paperback
$4.99 eBook

86 Sonnets for the 21st Century is a book of modern day poetry in which Mary Barnet writes of her challenges in life with family and friends. Illustrated by Richard E. Schiff.

Mary Barnet is a Nobel Prize nominee and the owner of the longest running poetry site on the internet. Richard E. Schiff contributed to, and appears in, the Academy Award winning documentary *Freeheld* now being made into a Feature Film.

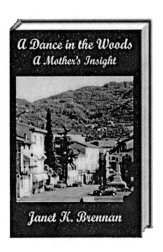

A Dance in the Woods: A Mother's Insight
Janet K. Brennan
ISBN: 978-1-937240-48-6
$15.95 Paperback
$5.99 eBook

A Dance in the Woods: A Mother's Insight is the true-life memoir of author and mother Janet Brennan seeking to come to terms with the loss of her daughter. When her husband is posted to Italy, Brennan must abruptly move and adjust to life in a strange new land. Yet her surroundings also possess indefinable healing power, as she journeys between her own memories and the comfort of the dark woods. She observes an old woman talking to her husband at his gravesite, listens to the practice music of a shed band, and experiences the mysterious, vibrant power of nature. *A Dance in the Woods* is a cathartic story of heartbreak, hope, and love, highly recommended.
-- Susan Bethany, Midwest Book Review.

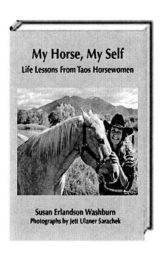

My Horse, My Self: Life Lessons from Taos Horsewomen

Susan Erlandson Washburn

ISBN: 978-1-937240-40-0

$13.95 Paperback

$5.99 eBook

My Horse, My Self: Life Lessons from Taos Horsewomen is a collection of intimate interviews with eighteen passionate and self-reliant horsewomen living in Northern New Mexico. Speaking from the heart, they describe the ways their horses have sustained them through trauma, forced them to discover strengths---and weaknesses---they didn't know they had, and helped them develop the confidence to become more truly themselves. The interviews are accompanied by photographic portraits that convey the essence of each woman's story and depict the stark beauty of Taos' high desert surroundings.

All I Can Gather & Give
Patti Tana
ISBN: 978-1-937240-45-5
$13.95 Paperback
$4.99 eBook

"All I Can Gather & Give" is a book of seventy-five poems by Patti Tana that is composed of three sections: "The
Ally You Have Chosen," "Imperfect Circles," and "Every
Season Has Its Beauty." This ninth collection of poems is
a tribute to the poet's sources of inspiration in nature and
the people she loves. In a voice intimate and accessible,
Tana finds words to transcend adversity and affirm a life
that is passionately lived.

Over Exposed
Terri Muuss
ISBN: 978-1-937240-23-3
$13.95 Paperback
$4.99 eBook

In the pages that follow, Muuss brings us close to
what we might describe as the secret war, the intimate
war, which resides in closed rooms, in seemingly ordinary
homes. Yet these poems are written, reader, with such del-
icacy, such concern for image, for pause, and purpose-for,
in fact, beauty.

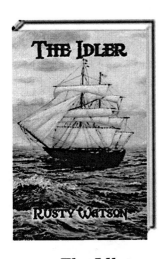

The Idler
Rusty Watson
ISBN: 978-1-937240-43-1
$14.95 Paperback
$4.99 eBook

Jeremiah Watts, in a drunken stupor, signs a seaman certificate and suddenly finds himself aboard the Ann Alexander, a rickety whaling ship. While aboard this ship, he begins a transformation as he gains maturity and begins to resolve his authority figure issues. This story is drawn from his journal and love letters covering the years he spent aboard the Ann Alexander.

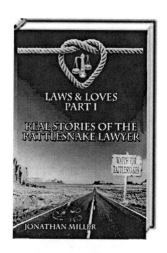

Laws and Loves
Jonathan Miller
ISBN: 978-1-937240-41-7
$14.95 Paperback
$5.99 eBook

Laws & Loves contains the real stories of the Rattle-snake Lawyer. Jonathan Miller is a practicing criminal defense attorney in New Mexico and the author of eight books. These are the chronicles of his early years, how he learned to balance the law with literature, all while looking for love in all the wrong courtrooms. This book is a must for anyone thinking of practicing law or falling in love.

Notes

CPSIA information can be obtained
at www.ICGtesting.com
Printed in the USA
FSOW02n0004281216
28888FS